shut up and up
and
LIVE!
(you know how)

AVERY
a member of
Penguin Group (USA) Inc.
New York

shut up and up
LIVE!
(you know how)

A 93-YEAR-OLD'S GUIDE FOR LIVING TO A RIPE OLD AGE

Marion P. Downs
M.A., DHS, HON. D.SC.

Published by the Penguin Group

Penguin Group (USA) Inc., 375 Hudson Street, New York, New York 10014, USA • Penguin Group (Canada), 90 Eglinton Avenue East, Suite 700, Toronto, Ontario M4P 2Y3, Canada (a division of Pearson Penguin Canada Inc.) • Penguin Books Ltd, 80 Strand, London WC2R 0RL, England • Penguin Ireland, 25 St Stephen's Green, Dublin 2, Ireland (a division of Penguin Books Ltd) • Penguin Group (Australia), 250 Camberwell Road, Camberwell, Victoria 3124, Australia (a division of Pearson Australia Group Pty Ltd) • Penguin Books India Pvt Ltd, 11 Community Centre, Panchsheel Park, New Delhi–110 017, India • Penguin Group (NZ), 67 Apollo Drive, Rosedale, North Shore 0632, New Zealand (a division of Pearson New Zealand Ltd) • Penguin Books (South Africa) (Pty) Ltd, 24 Sturdee Avenue, Rosebank, Johannesburg 2196, South Africa

Penguin Books Ltd, Registered Offices: 80 Strand, London WC2R 0RL, England

First Avery edition 2007
Previously self-published, in 2005
Copyright © 2005 by Marion P. Downs

Published simultaneously in Canada

Most Avery books are available at special quantity discounts for bulk purchase for sales promotions, premiums, fund-raising, and educational needs. Special books or book excerpts also can be created to fit specific needs. For details, write Penguin Group (USA) Inc. Special Markets, 375 Hudson Street, New York, NY 10014.

Library of Congress Cataloging-in-Publication Data

Downs, Marion P.
Shut up and live! (you know how) : a 93-year-old's guide
for living to a ripe old age / Marion P. Downs.
p.   cm.
ISBN 978-1-58333-292-4
1. Aging—Popular works.   2. Older people—Health and hygiene—Popular works.   I. Title.
RA777.6.D69   2007   2007028116
613′.0438—dc22

Printed in the United States of America
1   3   5   7   9   10   8   6   4   2

Book design by Stephanie Huntwork

Neither the publisher nor the author is engaged in rendering professional advice or services to the individual reader. The ideas, procedures, and suggestions in this book are not intended as a substitute for consulting with a physician. All matters regarding health require medical supervision. Neither the author nor the publisher shall be liable or responsible for any loss or damage allegedly arising from any information or suggestion in this book.

While the author has made every effort to provide accurate telephone numbers and Internet addresses at the time of publication, neither the publisher nor the author assumes any responsibility for errors, or for changes that occur after publication. Further, the publisher does not have any control over and does not assume any responsibility for author or third-party websites or their content.

With thanks to my children,

JODY PIKE, GEORGE DOWNS, AND SARA VOORHEES,

for their help, encouragement, support—and love.

And to

JIM SAVIERS,

certified strength and conditioning specialist,

National Strength and Conditioning Association

(my Marquis de Sade), for keeping me going.

CONTENTS

I took my first skiing lesson on my fiftieth birthday. My children had left for college or marriage, and there was a lot of expensive ski equipment in the closets. I figured somebody should be using that equipment, and it might as well be—*me*. I'd been an amateur athlete (really amateur) all my life, and after about twenty lessons, I learned how to turn and stop and snowplow, and ski down the fall line.

But on my fifty-first birthday, I was standing at the top of a black-diamond, or expert, slope and I was afraid to go down the hill.

"I can't do this!" I whined to the instructor. "It's too steep for me. What can I do?"

"Shut up and ski," the instructor answered. "You know how."

Since then, whenever I find myself apprehensive about doing something that seems too difficult, like driving in California traffic, I say to myself, "Shut up and drive! You know how."

Now, if I hear any protests from any of you that you're just too old to do the things I'm about to outline, all I can say to you is:

Shut up and live! You know how.

CHAPTER 1

finding the way

SO THIS IS WHAT HAS HAPPENED

In spite of illness, in spite even of the archenemy sorrow, one can remain alive long past the usual date of disintegration if one is unafraid of change, insatiable in intellectual curiosity, interested in big things, and happy in small ways.

—Edith Wharton, *A Backward Glance*

When I was seventy-two, I was sure I was going to die. I wasn't sick, and all of my appendages were intact, but both my parents died at seventy-two,

> Age doesn't matter
> unless you are cheese.
>
> —*Billy Burke*

and I had been convinced for many years that dying was the thing to do at seventy-two. In fear, I went to a psychiatrist to determine whether I was really being called upon to check out. The psychiatrist told me that it was a good thing I'd come to see him, as there was indeed a well-known psychiatric phenomenon known as the anniversary syndrome: many people have died on the precise date on which some family member or loved one has died. Then he assured me that it was not required of me to toe up at this time. He reminded me of the great differences between modern medicine and the primitive medicine practiced only a generation ago, of the changes in diet, the changes in lifestyle, and the improved environment. In fact, he said, looking me over, "You have every chance of living to a hundred!"

Oddly enough, that was worse news to me than a death sentence. I had, without thinking, modeled my life after my parents': I had read the books they read, espoused their politics, and after retirement, I had traveled as they had. Unwittingly, I had anticipated that my life would end, as theirs had, at seventy-two. Suddenly, here I was with no road map to direct me to—horrors!—possibly one hundred years.

So I said to him, "But I have no guidelines to live that long. How am I going to know how to live for the next twenty-eight years?" He replied, with a little smirk on his face, "That, my dear, is something you're going to have to work out for yourself."

STRANDED!

There I was—alive—and without the faintest idea what was going to happen to me next, hoping for the troops to come and rescue me. Alas, the Marines were otherwise engaged, and I would have to go it alone. I thought of the doctor on Mount Everest, buried in the snow with

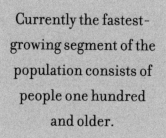

Currently the fastest-growing segment of the population consists of people one hundred and older.

no one to rescue him. He survived, and perhaps I could, too. Take one day at a time, I thought.

And now, following that formula, I've made it to ninety-three, with a clear blueprint of where I've been and how I got there. I'm not alone. Most of us are living longer than our parents did, many of us with no guidelines to see us through these critical years. For those who find themselves without a clear picture of how to live from wherever they are to wherever they're going, I offer this road map. This map is not only for old folks. Younger colleagues I meet at audiology conferences and younger women I've played tennis with—all of them "girls" in their forties, fifties, sixties, seventies, and eighties—often tell me, "You're my role model: what's your secret?"

This is an attempt to answer their questions. It seems I have a role to play, and play it I will.

HOW IT IS: LIFE AT NINETY-THREE

I wake up after seven hours of sleep interrupted by infrequent bathroom visits (helped by surgical bladder repair), breathe in my inhalants for my COPD (chronic obstructive pulmonary disease, or smoker's lungs; I had smoked until age fifty-five), loosen up my hip bursitis, put in my partial (nicely anchored to my tooth implants), put reading glasses on over my 20/20 vision (thanks to surgically implanted plastic lenses), put drops into my drying eyes, do a quick head maneuver (to eliminate dizziness associated with benign paroxysmal positional vertigo), stick my hearing aids into my ears, take my high-blood-pressure pills and my Premarin, then an Aleve for all my arthritic joints, then my Nexium for the reflux that causes my cough, do my Theraband therapy for my torn shoulder ligaments, place a Band-Aid on another bloody scuff of my sun-fragiled skin, check on the healed sutures of my recent brain-tumor surgery and on my facial precancerous healing spots, change the bandage on my leg's skin cancer, do my stretches, and lift my weights; then I look in the obit column, and if I'm not there, I breathe a thankful prayer to modern medicine and go out and play tennis. If it's winter, I may head for the ski slopes. I go very slowly, of course. But I go.

That's what it's all about: how to deal with all the ailments of old age. Forget about them, and get a life! Not only that, though you may not think it possible—get a life that's dashing, exuberant, a little crazy, but also one that becomes a model for all those sixty-five-year-olds who think that the fun life ends at sixty-five. It includes good sex, lots of exercise, close friends, capable doctors, intelligent eating, and a touch of the extreme.

Laughter is the key to survival.
The alternative is unacceptable.

A sense of humor has carried me through some agonizing years, having lost two husbands to Alzheimer's disease. During more than twenty years of caring for these men I have had to laugh at myself as often as I have laughed at them. You simply have to think it's funny when you find his dirty socks in the refrigerator, or the wastebasket used for a toilet, or all the clocks taken apart and the lamps dismantled. Or when you come into the room and he says, "Who in the world are you? Get the hell out!"

My favorite story is from my friend who had slept happily with her husband, who had Alzheimer's, but when they went downstairs to breakfast he spilled his OJ all over himself. As his wife tried frantically to clean him up, she railed at him harshly. "What a stupid thing to do—why can't you be more careful?" He looked at her and said plaintively, "Those people upstairs are much nicer than the people down here."

When dealing with these kinds of problems we always have to try to be "the people upstairs." We have a choice: to become bitter about how life has treated us or to see the humor in all the crazy cards life has dealt us. "Oh, poor me—the doctor says I have to have a hysterectomy. It's going to cost a lot, and I'll be down for months." Or: "I'm having a hysterectomy. They're taking out the nursery and leaving the playroom!"

Rebel against negative thinking. Remind yourself how wonderful it is that forty years ago an organ transplant would have meant moving a Hammond from one church to another. It is not acceptable to sit at home, watch television, damn the government or the world, and become a bitter old fart (or fartress?).

The older you get, the better you were.

Keeping one's mind busy is important, and I feel competent to talk about that, too. I had a busy career as a professor of audiology at Colorado Medical School, compiled some 130 articles in scientific journals, and coauthored three books. During the last year I've spoken at a few seminars, symposia, and professional meetings around the country, and one in Italy, one in Austria. I try to keep au courant about professional literature as well as current events.

I noticed a long time ago that one of the commonalities among people who've lived to eighty and are still lucid and sharp is that they're crossword puzzle fiends, so I became one. All three of my children and several grandchildren have already surpassed me on the Sunday *New York Times* puzzles, but I keep at it. Although the Friday and Saturday puzzles are impossible, I can still do the Monday, Tuesday, Wednesday, and Thursday puzzles. If I should ever find myself unable to do the Wednesday puzzle, I'm going to bring out the helium tank, à la the Hemlock Society's directions. (They've changed their name, I know, but I continue to call them Hemlock. I like their latest plan, to attach a tube from a helium tank to a plastic sack tied over your head and secured tightly around your neck. The only trouble is that I constantly use helium to blow up balloons for my great-grandchildren's birthday parties, and my supply may be exhausted by the time the crossword puzzles have decked me.)

Oh, yes, not only eleven grandchildren but also twenty-four (so far) great-grandchildren keep me mentally alert trying to remember all their names and what they want for Christmas. They all call me Granny, which is better than Nano or Pootsie or Gandy. It's to the point. Occasionally they call me Granola, which I permit if they precede it with "the Great."

Writing is one of the pleasures of life. Once you've accepted the fact that you're not Proust or Dorothy Parker and accept who you are, there's no writing block. I'm not Parker or Curie, I'm just an old gal with a good mind—not a great one— who's learned enough

> People living deeply
> have no fear of death.
> —*Anaïs Nin*

about life to pass it on. So bear with me. Actually, there's an analogy with life: once you realize you're not going to be Warren Buffett or Mel Gibson or Jennifer Lopez or Hillary Clinton, you can appreciate the fact that you've come this far intact, with a body that can do what you want it to and a mind whose greatness is in acceptance.

Many of our old friends are dropping out of life, both literally and figuratively. You haven't yet, and you don't have to anytime soon, or you wouldn't be reading this book. I hope to guide you into your nineties and even your hundreds. So let's go for it! The essential thing is that you take full responsibility for your own life.

DON'T DEPEND ON YOUR GENES!

The Harvard report on aging states that your genes are responsible for only twenty-five to thirty-five percent of your longevity. They are also responsible for only thirty percent of your physiological changes. So genes are not as important as we had thought. The really significant thing, of course, is to aim for a high quality of life while we're here, not how long we'll be hanging around.

Are you up to taking responsibility for that seventy percent that YOU, and you alone, are accountable for?

Don't rail against getting older, and don't complain about your aches and pains.

Shut up and live!
(You know how.)

CHAPTER 2

taking care
of the ol' bod'

Whatever the problem, exercise is always part of the solution. —J. D. Voorhees, M.D.

I had a head start on fitness because I was brought up in a little German town in Minnesota that had been founded by Turners. The Turnverein is a German organization whose motto is *Mens sana in corpore sano*—A sound mind in a sound body. I started gymnasium at four years old and practically lived there until I left for college. The weight started piling on then, and I've fought that battle ever since. Once my three children were raised, I started to exercise again, and I've never stopped since. Walking, running, cycling, tennis, swimming, skiing—and once a year I play golf just to remind myself what a better game tennis is.

The three most important factors in
a good and long life are:

1. Exercise
2. Exercise
3. Exercise

Everyone hates to exercise; we've become a nation of sofa softies. I hate to exercise, I admit, but I make it a priority every day for a half hour to two hours. It gives me the feeling of being twenty years old, and that is worth the effort. It simply has to be the number-one priority every day.

> But I hate to exercise.

One of the advantages of exercising is that it shows your best features to advantage. Got good legs? Wear tights as you walk or run or push weights in the gym. If you're a man with a great torso, go topless for all exercises. Got a good fanny? Show it off with tights. Got great boobs? I don't recommend topless for women (by this time, gravity has taken over all the vulnerable parts), but there are plenty of classy tops to show off a good chest. As a woman, I'm quite aware that certain men have favorite female attributes. Some men are leg men, some are bosom men, and some are fanny men. My misfortune is that both of my husbands were fanny men, and I don't have any. Legs, yes; fanny, no. But show off what you have.

If you already exercise, do more. If you don't, you're never too old to start. The news is full of stories of people in their nineties beginning to lift weights and to walk miles, with resulting increased strength and endurance.

nutrition

According to an old saying, we are what we eat.

I wouldn't touch nutrition with a ten-foot pole. A thousand and one diets are out there, and anything I say would only confuse the issue. If you don't know how to eat properly, nothing I can tell you will help.

All right—you twisted my arm. My diet consists of:

High protein
Low carbohydrates
Lots of fruit
Force-feeding veggies

Enough already.

THE PROGRAM

If you don't already, go regularly to a gym or find a personal trainer to come into your home. My trainer has a B.S. in exercise science and is a certified senior trainer. It's a good idea to have a qualified trainer who understands the problems of seniors. Any trainer you choose should be certified by at least one of the big three: the National Strength and Conditioning Association; the American College of Sports Medicine; or the American Council on Exercise.

I call my trainer the "Marquis de Sade" and claim that he is a certified sadist, because he pushes me mercilessly to do more every time. How can I complain, though, when I see the results? He has given me a triad of exercises, and I recommend them highly:

1. Stretching: every day, first thing in the morning (15 to 20 minutes).
2. Strengthening: three times a week (1 hour).
3. Aerobics: four times a week (1 to 2 hours).

All three of these exercises are necessary to giving the ol' bod' what it needs. Here's an outline of what they entail:

stretches

Back exercises: Absolutely essential! Your trainer will show you a number of exercises that will strengthen your back and eliminate that unforgiving pain that comes with back trouble. If you've ever suffered from back pain, you know; you really want to end it all, after months of unrelenting stabs every time you move. I know that feeling: when I was thirty-six years old, one of my daughters, at five years old, had measles encephalitis, which required almost constant swabbing with cool water to keep the fever down. It meant more than a week of bending over and lifting her, and it ended up with her recovering and my back suffering.

The ever helpful surgeons marked me for a spinal fixation operation, and I was scheduled to go under the knife. Then I remembered what one of my old-time doctor relatives once said: "Never let anyone do anything to your back." I canceled the surgery and embarked on the first of many therapeutic routines, which included some of the kinds of exercises I am recommending.

If you haven't yet learned the fundamental truism that a good back depends on a strong stomach, etch it now in your memory. Strong stomach muscles relieve the back from doing all the work. So you will have several routines of crunches (repeated many times), bicycle-type movements, and other sadistic tummy-strengthening exercises. Do them in whatever protocol your trainer recommends. My trainer has no pity on me. But it's worth it.

Specific back-strengthening groups will include supine (knees bent to chin, knees rolling to side, hip raising) and prone (hip-raising, head and feet raised). Always, when on your back, lift up your hips so that your back is flat against the floor, otherwise the back has to strain to do the movements. Your sadist will devise other movements. Don't do any of them until he or she feels you can do them safely!

Believe me, these things work. Since my initial episode, I have not had a single pang in my back for fifty-four years. The back may feel a bit stiff in the morning, but the workout soon clears things up.

body stretches

Sitting up on the floor, legs extended, you will do at least five minutes of different leg stretches. Every stretch must be held up to thirty seconds, and it is imperative that the entire time you should maintain good posture—a straight back—during stretches. There are other exercises to stretch your upper legs as well as the lower ones—just follow your guru's advice.

Neck and shoulder stretches: Most of us develop arthritic necks when we age, and we forget that for the neck, like every other arthritic joint, exercise is the key. Turning your head to the side, then lowering and raising the head in that position, must be done every day. Be sure to have your guru check that you're doing it right. Roll the shoulders backward, together and singly. Do it while you're walking and sitting, many times a day, whenever you think of it.

These are the exercises that keep you looking young as you walk and sit. You know the picture of the old person, shuffling along in short steps, head bent down and forward. It's the old folks' shuffle. The reason is that people's leg muscles get short and weak, and in order to locomote they take small shuffling steps. The leg stretches you do daily will allow you to stride, not shuffle, by throwing your leg forward as you walk, and taking longer steps. Your stretches will guarantee that you walk young!

And what about your posture as you walk and sit? The shoulder and neck exercises will let you hold your head high and your shoulders back. Chin in, plebe! Keep the posture when you sit, too. Don't do the computer crunch.

My father had been in the army, and even in his seventies he would stride down the street, head erect, and you could almost hear "The Stars and Stripes Forever" being played overhead. Get your own Sousa band going!

strengthening

The wrong kind of strengthening exercises can do damage to your bones and muscles, so I will leave the specifics to your expert trainer. Be sure your expert trainer *is* an expert.

A Johns Hopkins study reports that walking, swimming, cycling, and exercise machines don't prevent bone loss. Impact exercises protect the bones best: jogging, jumping rope, step aerobics, and especially strength training. They recommend weights that add as much as ten to fifteen percent of your body weight for squats, lunges, and calf raises. These help strengthen the bones, especially the hips, which are particularly vulnerable for older people. Be sure to check with your doctor to make sure that your knee joints will take the stresses. For arm bones, biceps curls, chest presses, and lateral raises do the trick.

I have my own observation: Fast, vigorous walking has to be good for the bones. The heels strike the ground with quite an impact, much like jogging. So, Johns Hopkins, I have spoken!

My exercise toys include:

Weights: From 1 pound to 20 pounds—so far. My Marquis de Sade is threatening to get 30-pound weights, especially for knee bending, lunges, and steps-up-and-down. The lighter weights I use for elbow bends and arm raises. Because I have torn rotator cuffs on both shoulders, I can do only light weights on lifting straight up without pain. But I'm working on it: every month I try to increase by a pound. It's slow going.

Those rotator cuffs have given me fits for years. My sports orthopod told me that surgery would give me only a fifty-fifty chance of adequate use, and it would take six months to recover. Well, I didn't like those odds, and I figured I didn't have six months to give out

of the rest of my life, so I opted for physical therapy. Those exercises I still do every day, despite my doctor's saying it was hopeless. I even serve the occasional ace.

The docs aren't always right. When I fell on the tennis court five years ago and tore one of the muscles in my left shoulder, the doc said that I would never again be able to throw up a tennis ball for the serve, nor have much use for it. But my Marquis de Sade set up a rope pulley the next day so I would keep the range of motion in that arm, and started the strengthening of the other muscles to compensate for the lost one. Before long, I could throw the ball straight up, and now I can do almost anything with that arm. It just won't allow me to put heavy dishes up on the shelf, or push to the side when my elbow is held at my hip.

Everything else, okay. Remember: "Whatever the problem, exercise is always part of the solution." In my case, it was the WHOLE solution!

Therabands: Yellow, red, green, blue, black, and gray—I have them all—one for every degree of difficulty, secured on the door. I use them mainly for my shoulder therapy, but also for strengthening. Putting a rod through a loop and pulling down in different ways is excellent strengthening for the arm and shoulder muscles.

If your sports orthopod recommends a physical therapist regimen, go for it. Your trainer can then work those exercises into his other strengthening routine. You will note that I say "sports orthopod." I used to go to a regular orthopedist, who usually recommended six months of rest for any of my sports-related problems—something that is anathema to me. A sports orthopedist, on the other hand, will work with you on what you can do to keep going. For one shoulder tear he let me go ahead and play tennis, but said to serve underhanded for six weeks and let every overhead ball fall low enough to take it almost from the ground up. And gave me a Theraband routine as well. I like that.

 **Large balance ball:** Although balancing is a big problem for me, with my BPPV (benign paroxysmal positional vertigo), it's fun to work with a balance ball. BPPV occurs when the little "rocks" in the ear lose their attachments and go wandering into the wrong semicircular canals. Fortunately, the dizziness that results can easily be cured by a good vestibular expert—read about it in Chapter 6. My balance is excellent now, after lots of work on the ball along with other balancing routines. The ball is also used for strengthening by rolling forward and back on it.

Soccer ball: Usually I use it against the wall, for wall push-ups, or rolling it up and down and around for shoulder work. And for some reason, my Marquis de Sade decided I had to learn how to play soccer, which was nonexistent in my day, so I never learned to kick. But he figured it would help my balance to kick the soccer ball back and forth, so now, at ninety-three, I know how to play soccer.

aerobics

Be sure to get your doctor's permission to start any program of strenuous aerobics. But do start one if you haven't already. You have a choice:

- Running
- Bicycling
- Swimming
- Treadmill
- Health club machines
- Walking

My preference is running, as once you are a runner it's hard to slow down and walk. But I have had to slow down, and I find walking is a great option, recommended by most health experts. It helps the lungs and heart, which are rather important in longevity.

I started running in earnest when I was fifty-nine. By weeks, first I ran two blocks, then four, then eight, then twelve. After one mile I found I could do two handily, and I'll never forget celebrating my sixtieth birthday doing three. It took thirty-five minutes. When I was seventy, it took forty-five minutes, and when I was eighty, it took fifty-five. After that, my lungs couldn't stand the constant running, so I walked half the time and ran the other half. By eighty-five I was walking two-thirds of the time, and by eighty-nine, three-quarters. I now settle for ninety-five percent walking and run as much as I can.

However, cross training beckons, and bicycling is attractive as a second aerobic option. To my great disgust, my doctor and my family won't let me do two-wheel bicycling because of my benign paroxysmal positional vertigo. So, ignominy of ignominies, I bought a three-wheel recumbent bike, which seems to take even more effort than a two-wheeler, especially on the hills. It satisfies aerobic requirements.

The other options for aerobics are great, but I haven't tried them. And then there are specialty training programs, like Pilates, Curves, and others. I'm sure they are great, but I really like to do everything in my own home and at my own speed. My trainer proved his worth many times over, by giving me the special exercises that improved the problems I developed.

When two old people get together, they always have that organ recital. It's "How is your bladder? My stomach is giving me fits. I had ten skin scruffs last week. How many precancerous lesions do *you* have?" etc. I want to change this scenario. Let's say, instead: "How many miles did you do today? Is your bicycle in good shape? My trainer upped my weights to thirty pounds. Did you play tennis [or golf] today? My serve is getting better," etc. As Maya Angelou says, "I may have pains, but I don't have to be one myself!"

Shut up and walk!
(You know how.)

Winning in a National Senior Games
Over-90 tournament

NEWS ON THE BENEFITS
OF EXERCISE

More research has been reported indicating that vigorous exercise can create new brain cells as well as it can build muscles and prevent heart disease. Great news for us seniors! We know we've been losing brain cells since we were forty; now we know that we can rebuild them. Studies have focused on aerobic exercise, because the few reports on stretching, toning, and weightlifting have not found significant effects on cognition. Lest we throw out those latter routines, remember that unless all of your muscles are flexible and strong, you won't be able to do the vigorous aerobics required to improve your cognition.

A University of Illinois study on third- and fifth-graders found that the kids with the best brains were the ones who had the fittest bodies. So get your children or grandchildren out on the soccer field, the baseball diamond, the basketball court, or into the swimming pool—and if possible, go with them. You'll be raising future brain surgeons, astronauts, and audiologists.

A case can be made that exercise may prevent Alzheimer's disease or other dementias, although it may be difficult to prove. At any rate, a strong, flexible body is essential to build an active and productive mind.

Running and/or fast walking are the necessary ingredients, and how much you should do depends on the size and quality of your own body. Ask your trainer for advice on this. I find that I can fast-walk for three miles every day when I'm not playing tennis. It takes me about fifty minutes to do the three miles if I'm in good condition. In the old days it took me thirty-five minutes, running. No, I don't look back with envy—I know that I just have to be at the top of my form for my age. Getting to the top is the goal.

SEX AND EXERCISE

And now comes a study of 2,126 men, published in February 2007 in the *American Journal of Medicine*, showing that men with ED (I'm still too Victorian to spell it out, but here, I will: it's "erectile dysfunction") reported doing less strenuous exercise than did others. There was also a relationship between less exercise and higher risks for hypertension, poor cholesterol, and diabetes.

So if you're a man with ED, and you want a good sex life, get off your duff and exercise. Your wife should also be motivated to get you out there, and it wouldn't hurt her to accompany you.

THE LURE OF INVALIDISM

A skiing injury introduced me to the seduction of being an invalid. It caused me to have a great empathy with people who have chosen chronic invalidism. There I was, flat on my back, unable to walk, surrounded by solicitous friends and family. Why should I start exercise for my legs when I could be wheeled around easily in a wheelchair? Why should I go to a pool to exercise in the water when I was being waited on by those sympathetic friends? Why should I try to get around in a walker when people were cooking delicious meals for me? Why spoil their loving ministrations? For a short time, I was tempted by that life and fully understood why someone would choose that path. What awakened me from that dream? It was my Marquis de Sade, who yelled: *"Shut up and get off your butt!"*

And I did. It was agony, but worth every minute: going to the pool every day to get those limbs moving easily, doing exercises in bed, on chairs, standing up, against the wall. One benefit was being so tired at night that I slept marvelously, but the greatest reward of all was coming back to the same world I had left and being an active part of a life that has no limits. But for those few moments, I had realized why someone would be seduced by the choice of leaving it behind.

Too many people are thinking of security instead of opportunity; they seem to be more afraid of life than death.

CHAPTER 3

and then there's your mind

As if, one by one, the memories you used to harbor decided to retire to the southern hemisphere of the brain, to a little fishing village where there are no phones. —Billy Collins

You go to the refrigerator to get some butter for your bread, and stand there, looking inside without a clue about what you came for. "Yikes!" you scream. "I'm getting Alzheimer's!" Stop and think: Didn't you do the same thing when you were twenty, and thought nothing of it? Such lapses have been common all our lives, but now they seem of great concern.

When you were in college, you couldn't introduce your best friend to someone because the name was somewhere else. Now you do the same thing and worry about it. Perhaps we do it a little more often now that we're older, but be of good cheer. There is a name for it: benign senescent forgetfulness. Focus on the word *benign*.

As for short-term memory, some researchers have found that the ability to remember newly acquired information depends on the same faculties used to retrieve memories from long ago—something that most older people do with great ease. So if someone can tell stories about his youth, he also has the faculty to do the same for recent events. And if he can't, sometimes it's a *failure to pay attention* rather than an inability to learn. What can we do to improve that attention and our overall memory at this stage of life?

"Use it or lose it" is more true for your mind than for any other part of your body.

We *can do a great deal to improve our memory:*

The most important thing you can do for your brain is aerobic exercise. The research reported in Chapter 2 showed that we can actually grow new brain cells by doing regular aerobics; this will make us smarter as well as healthier.

- Be physically active. The old brain needs blood to get to it so it can function better. Regular exercise pumps more blood into the brain and improves its function. Go to that chapter and *do what it says!*
- Be mentally active. You may have retired, and don't have the stimulation of your work and your associates. Substitute all that with daily activities.
- Break down your thoughts. Telephone numbers and Social Security numbers are broken down into sections because they're easier to remember that way. Do that with your checking account number or any list you want to memorize.

- Use hearing, vision, and feeling. Talk out loud to yourself while locking the door, putting something down, remembering what you're supposed to do next—this always reinforces the action you want to remember. You can write things down, or even draw a rough picture, and use touch to emphasize what you want to remember. Always repeat a name out loud after you've been introduced to some-one new.

- Employ mnemonics. Make up a sentence or a story to remember lists of words or names. For example, if asked to remember "apple, tree, pencil, boy," you can imagine "An apple lay under a tree next to a boy who was writing with a pencil." For names like Alice, Norma, John, Sydney, imagine "Alice in Wonderland sits next to Norma Rae in St. John's Church in Sydney, Australia." This will help you re-member, as well as exercise your brain.

- Take time. When learning something new, don't try to memorize it all at once. Go back to it several times a day, every day. To memorize a talk, go over it once every hour or so.

- Write things down. Make use of appointment books, calendars, Post-its, and notebooks. We accumulate so much garbage in our brains that we can't be expected to remember all the new things that are piling up. Keep a pen and a notebook handy wherever you are.

- Think active aging. It's not true that age always slows our cognitive processes and makes us forget things. We can keep our minds just as active as ever by doing the strategies outlined here. Just believe!

- Do the *New York Times* crossword puzzle. "Oh, I can't do that," I hear you say. Yes, you can. Start with the Monday puzzle, and work until you get it. It may take a whole day, but do it. Then try the Tuesday puzzle and do the best you can. Then next week, Wednesday's, and so on. Don't even try the Saturday puzzle, but start working on the Sunday one, which is a wonderful challenge, with some fascinating intellectual machinations. Remember what Churchill said: Never give in!

- Play games. Scrabble is stimulating. It makes you think. So does any kind of Trivial Pursuit. Bridge is great. Take classes in Ping-Pong or golf or tennis or croquet, and whip up your competitive spirit.
- Read, read, read. Develop an opinion about what you read, and tell people about it. Argue for your viewpoint. Try to tell friends a brief synopsis of the book, and remember almost verbatim a particularly impressive passage.
- Study a foreign language, and go to that country to try it out. Mexico is close, so study Spanish and go across the border.
- Learn to play a musical instrument: piano, recorder, cello, whatever grabs you. Then see if you can play with a group and *make music.*
- Start a new hobby: knitting, woodworking, raising dogs, raising hell.
- Volunteer at a charity or hospital. Think of how good you'll feel about yourself.

- Keep up your social interactions. See old friends as well as develop new ones. Invite them to your house for dinner or games.
- Have two alcoholic drinks a day if you are a man, one if you are a woman. (Oh, happy day!) Yes, a research study showed the risk of cognitive impairment was reduced in those who consumed those small quantities of alcohol. Any more than that increased the risk of impairment, however, so watch it. (One drink can be 12 ounces of beer, or 5 ounces of wine, or 1.5 ounces of spirits.)
- Play memory games. Challenge yourself by seeing how many telephone numbers you can memorize; how many numbers you can repeat after hearing them; do your addition, subtraction, and multiplication tables as you go to sleep. And buy some of the good memory books in the bookstore: *The Memory Bible*, for example. In any case, the worst thing you can do if you think you're becoming forgetful is to

complain to everyone around you about how forgetful you're becoming.

ON DECISIONS

When faced with making a decision, I've always believed that it doesn't really matter which alternative you choose: either one will turn out to your best advantage if you embrace it. A case in point is how I got into the audiology profession.

In fifteen years, I had raised three children. One day, at age thirty-five, I was doing the dishes, when I had my epiphany: Was this what I was going to do for the rest of my life? I, who had been a valedictorian, and Phi Beta Kappa in my junior year of college? No way.

I had read in the paper that the University of Denver was enrolling students for the fall semester. Why not me? I dried my hands, took off my apron, and hurried over to the big arena where registration was taking place.

It was 1947, and thousands of soldiers who had returned from World War II were taking advantage of the GI Bill and registering. The lines for each graduate department stretched out for what seemed like miles. My children would be home from school in an hour—I'd never make it! But wait—one line was shorter than any of the others. I might make that one in time. So I joined the shortest line and soon found myself registering for speech pathology and audiology. So what if I'd never heard of audiology? So what if I'd only seen the words "speech pathology" a few years before? I would now start studying in this field.

My first course was anatomy, which I loved, and it involved a lot of memorization. When the final exam came, all the other students left after an hour of writing, but I was just beginning. I had studied so hard and knew so much that I couldn't stop writing. The professor came to me and said, "I'll give you ten more minutes, but that's all." Fortunately I finished in time, and tied for the best score in the class. After all those years away from school, I had been so eager to learn that I'd gotten carried away with my own curiosity.

After that I calmed down and even once got as low a mark as a B+.

As it turned out, I was a natural for audiology. It required close association with people, and I love people. I was privileged to be able to help those who had hearing problems. Children were my specialty. I loved my own kids, and could easily love all comers.

In 1974, after twenty-three years of working as a clinical audiologist, I wrote these lines in a book on pediatric audiology, *Hearing in Children*, that I cowrote with J. L. Northern:

Another principle is to love every child as a human being. The clinician is often hard-put to develop any charitable feelings toward the wall-climber, the temper tantrum expert, the withdrawn "Great Stone Face," or in some cases the misshapen, contorted face and limbs of the syndrome-ridden child. On one of my first contacts with Crouzon's Syndrome, I was aghast at the little two-year-old with the great bulging eyes, high head, and malformed nose and wondered what resources of objectivity I could draw upon to relate to this blob for whom nature dealt a wicked blow. Suddenly, as I was hesitating, the blob smiled at me—a smile so deeply compassionate for me that I hugged him in the joy of recognition of mutual humanity. The same humanity under-lies the kicker, the screamer, the silent one—all of them humanly acting out their protests at a world that has given them less than it has to others. They too can be loved.

And I loved audiology. Still do.

As always, the rule is:
Shut up and live!
(You can remember how.)

My ninetieth birthday celebration—
attached to a handsome hunk!

live gloriously

Tell me, what is it you plan to do with your one wild and precious life? —Mary Oliver

Well, we've come this far, and we have every probability of going further. The strange thing is, the older we get, the longer our estimated life span is extended. Even at ninety, you have a better chance of living to a hundred than you did when you were eighty; the statistics on longevity prove that. So we have quite a few years ahead of us to live that wild and precious life. Here's where I have developed some personal philosophy:

I find nature becoming more precious the closer I come to joining it.

Every moment we have is priceless—even those seemingly endless moments waiting in traffic. Make them profitable by savoring everything you can see or feel or hear: faces of strangers in the street, the roar of the machine world, the comfort of the car seat. Open the window and let the whole busy world in. You are a precious part of it. Be here, NOW.

Allow yourself to feel *everything* more deeply. Let your favorite fugue come into yourself so deeply that it hurts. Let the sight of the alpenglow at sunset on your favorite mountain strike a blow to your heart that makes you cry. Hold the hand of someone you love for a cherished instant, and make it a forever moment. Make every moment a forever moment. These are the instants that we can take with us. They belong to us, and to no one else.

If you're a businessperson: "Yesterday is a canceled check; tomorrow is a promissory note; only today is negotiable." Negotiate today with all your inner funds.

SPIRITUALITY

If you're religious, you understand spirituality. Increase it every day that you live, deepening your relationship with your God. It is a profound source of strength that reduces the stress of living and brings you meaning. Work for serenity and contentment. You'll have that extra edge of living longer—and better.

If you're not religious, you can take strength from other aspects of spirituality, such as those defined by Thomas Friedman (author of *Longitudes and Attitudes*). He pointed to the terrorists, who believe that "our wealth and power are unrelated to anything in the soul of this country; that wealth and power can only be achieved by giving up your values. . . . This view misses the fact that American power and wealth flow from a deep spiritual source: a respect for the individual, a spirit of tolerance for differences of faith or politics, a respect for freedom of thought as the necessary foundation for all creativity, and a spirit of

unity that encompasses all kinds of differences."
Friedman believes that only a society with a deep spiritual energy, "which welcomes immigrants and worships freedom, could constantly renew itself and its sources of power and wealth."

Many of us have had mystical experiences that occur without warning, when suddenly time seems to stop, and the moment is beautiful and magical, lifting us above ourselves in a piercing instant of supreme awareness. It can happen when we are seeing an extraordinarily beautiful scene, or hearing a thrilling musical score, or just in an ordinary moment when we least expect it. When I was young, a dear aunt of mine asked me, "Do you ever feel a time in your life when you think, 'This is the moment!' and things stand still?" It was her way of expressing the mystical experience that has been described by some of the great mystics in religious history. It is something that we all can experience if we let ourselves open to recognize it. Spirituality is not exclusively the province of religious mentors. We can renew ourselves with these kinds of spiritual energy. Life becomes more wonderful, more precious, the older we get.

LUCK

The race is not to the swift, nor the battle to the strong, neither yet bread to the wise, nor yet riches to men of understanding, nor yet favor to men of skill; but time and chance happeneth to them all.

—Ecclesiastes 9:11

There's another word for it, and it's called *luck*. Even on the tennis court the game doesn't always go to the best player if luck is against him.

I should know. I've been lucky so many times it almost makes me believe in a guardian angel. Let me elaborate:

In 1969, I found myself teaching in Saigon, with an American Medical Association assistance program for the Vietnamese. Our sponsor, the minister of education, had taken us one Sunday night to examine the hearing of the prime minister (fifty percent of Vietnamese people had chronic otitis, or ear infection). I brought my audiometer and sound-level meter along to test his hearing. Afterward, the minister dropped us off at our lodgings and the instruments were left in his car. He was to pick us up the next day to go to the hospital for our teaching there. Unfortunately, shortly before he picked us up, a motorcyclist threw a grenade into the window of his car, killing him and his driver.

When I finally retrieved my instruments, the audiometer was a molten mass smaller than a soccer ball, and the sound-level meter was just a scrap of metal. If I had been in the car, I would have been a scrap of nothing! It's all about being in the right place at the right time.

And then there was the time when I was just twenty-one, with a three-month-old baby, near the Canadian border in Montana. My husband was doing geology in an oilfield, and we had a house twenty miles from the nearest town, heated by gas from the adjacent oil well. Everything was fine until the great December blizzard of 1935. Not your run-of-the-mill blizzard, but horizontal heavy blowing snow, zero visibility, and a temperature of 60 below.

We woke to find that the gas burner in the furnace wasn't functioning. The gas from the well had moisture in it, and the entire flow was frozen. There was nothing to do but bundle up and take our chances to find some warm shelter. Which we did.

We knew that about half a mile away was a one-room tarpaper shack where the oil-rig roustabout lived with his wife. But how to find it, when we were blinded by the snow? We walked out and tried to get our bearings, but it was useless. As we staggered around, my husband fell over a pipe, and he remembered that the same pipe went past the roustabout's shack. So we huddled together with the baby between us, my husband took hold of the pipe, and we started out.

Like orphans of the storm, we kept going—endlessly, it seemed, and despite our exhaustion. Then we saw something black through the snow; it was the shack. The roustabout and his wife let us in;

fortunately, they had a wood stove and plenty of wood to keep warm.

Six days later, the storm abated and cars could be dug out of the snowdrifts. We were taken to town, where we stayed in an apartment for the rest of the winter.

The luck? My husband's stumbling over that pipe led us to warmth. Otherwise . . .

Any more luck? Well, I consider myself lucky to have survived a plane crash out of Denver in 1975. We had just left the airport, were no more than a hundred feet in the air, when the pilot got an abort signal and had to drop down and crash-land in an open field. We hit the ground hard and careened into an electrical facility, and the plane started to burn.

I was in the front, an aisle seat, and was the first down the chute to safety. Seeing the flames that could have created an explosion, I ran so fast that I must have been a quarter-mile away before the next person got off the plane. But everyone got off, and only a few people had injuries. I was abashed to think that I had displayed no noble instincts of compassion for any of my fellow passengers—I'd just off and run.

Next time, I promise, I'll do better.

CURRENT EVENTS

What's going on in the world? This fascinates me more and more. From my perspective of never having seen an airplane until I was ten years old, and having ridden in a horse-drawn carriage at an early age, the times are a wondrous phenomenon. When I was in grade school, my brother got a crystal radio transmitter, and we listened, amazed, through the rough static, to the first radio station. And I still don't know if television is a blessing or a curse.

My interest in current events has, I think (and hope), helped to keep my mind active. I support a political party with zeal, and sometimes, with vehemence. It alienates me sometimes, but not much, from some of my friends who are just as zealous in their support of another party. But we avoid the subject as much as we can. I just say, "I will fight to the death for your right to be ignorant."

Oliver Wendell Holmes said, "Not to share in the activity and passion of your time is to count as not having lived. I don't claim virtue. I claim a low level of boredom." That's it: be bored unless you can participate in some way, even as an observer, in the things that are going on in the world.

Shut up and be passionate!
(You know how.)

CHAPTER 5

x-rated sex

And I think, if my memory serves me, there was nothing more fun than a man! —Dorothy Parker

L et us now praise the orgasm. Despised, kept secret, branded a dirty word, it is now coming into its own. Let us sing of it, extol it, rejoice in it, and burn incense in its honor. Without it, you and I would not be here, so why not glory in it?

Imagine, then, how delighted I was to read in the Harvard report on aging that the more orgasms one had, the longer one's life could be. A contribution to longevity? What a happy thought! And even further joy, the article stated that it matters not whether the orgasm is achieved *with* a partner, or without. Now, that is one thought that I hope I do not have to elaborate on for any of you. (If this offends your sensibilities, please read on no more.)

Medical journals are rife with studies about the benefits of orgasms. One of my favorites studied a thousand middle-aged men for ten years. They found that men who had the highest frequency of orgasm had a death rate *half* that of those who weren't as active. In a follow-up study, the researchers found that the men who had sex three or more times a week cut their risk of stroke or heart attack by fifty percent. Sex, they said, boosts production of testosterone, which leads to stronger bones and muscles. Now why haven't we seen such studies about women? We simply have to assume that these things apply to women, which might be a dubious assumption, I fear.

WOMEN

Most women I know enjoy the skin orgasms that come from gently rubbing the back or arms, or anywhere.

All the women in my family—some twenty-five of them—enjoy the family back rub. It may be a three- or four-cornered back rub, with everyone in a circle rubbing another's back, and oohs and aahs filling the air. Sounds perverse, but it's one of life's joys. I know of a hairdresser who can give a great head rub when washing hair, and he is in great demand.

In addition, we women have the classic orgasm. How lucky can we be!

MEN

We know (and I know from experience) that men vary widely in their ability—or their inclination—to have sex. Two of our ex-presidents are considered by many to be what we women would call sex-crazed. There are at least two theories about this condition: one psychological, the other physiological.

I hold with the physiological theory. Some men who have low testosterone levels also have low sex urges. These seem to be men who also are inclined to osteoporosis. And other men who evidently are high in testosterone have strong sex urges. This theory is bolstered by the fact that medical literature reports that testosterone deficiency in men is indeed associated with osteoporosis. The relationship to sex is hard to find in the literature. It is just my belief that the oversexed man is also over-testosteroned. I doubt that we will ever see the sex-crazed develop osteoporosis.

John F. Kennedy was quoted as saying that if he didn't have a woman every day he got a headache. Clinton, too, must have been simply driven by his testosterone. How they balanced that with the presidency is something we will never know!

I've never known a woman who was as driven by sex as some men are. Sex is so psychological in women that I tend to scoff at the theory that women can be driven by hormones. So much for that.

SEX AND OLD AGE

And now, let's hear it for Viagra!

I have no idea if or when one loses one's sex drive.

I'll let you know when I'm a hundred or a hundred ten. Who knows? From my limited experience up to now, it continues through the eighties and, I hope, the nineties. Nature would indeed be cruel if she deprived us of that as well as making us work like the devil for our sight, our hearing, our muscles, our bones, and our gray cells! Whether any men lose their sex drive in old age is something I haven't as yet experienced.

They say that Viagra is the old man's friend, but as you know, it only provides the mechanical ability to have sex. It doesn't provide the desire, the need to be with someone you love—which brings us to . . .

Love. You really don't have to have intercourse to make love. Intercourse is nice, but not always that easy. What is easy and comfortable is to take advantage of the largest organ in the human body: the skin. Skin contact, hugging, caressing, kissing are all prime surrogates for sex—providing the couple expresses caring and tenderness for each other.

We know that babies require their loving parents' touch, close holding, and hugging in order to thrive. The eminent psychiatrist Dr. René Spitz showed that children in orphanages, where there was little touching, not only failed to thrive and incurred permanent developmental retardation but also sometimes died prematurely. Died from lack of love!

We all need love, and a wonderful way to express it is to touch each other. Sex can be fulfilled just by holding each other closely and touching the skin, just as a mother holds the child. Holding hands can be exquisitely fulfilling, and to me it is almost a sacred thing to hold the hand of someone you love while they are dying. You can still fall in love at eighty, ninety, or a hundred. The feeling is always there, waiting for us. It will never die. There seems to be something in us that reaches out to be close to another person. It's worth reaching out . . . and out . . . and out.

> Age does not protect you from love, but love to some extent protects you from age.
>
> —*Jeanne Moreau*

RETROSPECT

Many criticisms have come forth about the sexual freedom that arose after the liberating sixties. That freedom is being blamed for the increase in divorce, sexual promiscuity, teenage pregnancies, HIV, marital infidelity, and casual living arrangements. It certainly is a change from the Victorian environment I grew up in. All my mother ever told me about sex was that a woman just had to submit to a man's urges, without any thought of enjoyment for her. Fortunately, by the time she told me that I already knew better. The openness of sex today is to me an emancipation from that prudish era. The pendulum may have swung pretty far, but I suspect it will return to a rational point. Perhaps HIV has already moderated much excess. I have faith that good sense will prevail, as in all things.

ADVICE ON SEX

There's a discovery about some animals and birds that mate for life. It seems that in addition to making the original mating displays, honks, and noises to interest and secure their mates, they periodically repeat all the displays and noises, complete with feather ruffling, tail spreading, and loud honking, just to renew their mutual attraction for each other. I hardly think I have to elaborate on this. But please, from time to time, ruffle your tail feathers and *honk!*

Don't complain that you're too old
for sex or love. Shut up and honk!
(You know how.)

CHAPTER 6

becoming your own medical expert

ARE YOU A MEDICAL SOPHISTICATE?

Many of my friends and acquaintances have had unnecessarily bad outcomes from surgery or disease because they chose the wrong health specialist. Their experiences convinced me that in order to keep functioning well, one must first become sophisticated about medicine and medical practice. Not to do so may mean unnecessary physical problems, and even early death. An article in the *Journal of Personality and Social Psychology* describes a research investigation that concludes: "Caring for your own health over a lifetime is a difficult and demanding job, and not everyone is smart enough to do it well. 'Health Literacy' predicts outcomes, even after social class is controlled for."

You don't have to be a genius to be "smart enough," but you do have to devote time and study to learning how to take care of your own body. Diligence, as well as intelligence, will dictate how well and how long you live.

Take the following test to determine whether you have the basic knowledge to take care of yourself in the maze of today's medical establishment. All the questions involve elementary familiarity with medicine and medical practice.

1. Do you know how and when to do the Heimlich maneuver?
2. Could you do CPR in an emergency?
3. Do you know your complete cholesterol profile, and the difference between HDL and LDL?
4. Do you know all the factors that can cause dizziness?

5. Do you know the symptoms of a heart attack for women? For men?

6. Do you know the symptoms of a stroke and the one most important thing to do?

7. Do you know all the possible treatments for arthritis?

8. Do you know the symptoms of Alzheimer's disease?

9. Do you know the difference between asthma, emphysema, and COPD (smoker's lungs)?

10. Do you know what your bone density is, and its relation to osteoporosis?

See pages 84–99 for answers. Count 10 points for each answer you got right.

> 90 to 100 is an A.
> 80 to 89 is a B.
> 70 to 79 is a C.
> 60 to 69 is a D.

If you scored less than 60, you need to read the rest of this chapter and go back to school!

A bonus question to raise your score by ten percent, if you get everything right: Do you know what the following physicians or surgeons do, how to find them, and which ones are the best in your area?

    a. Internist or family practitioner
    b. Cardiologist
    c. Orthopedist
    d. Ophthalmologist
    e. Otolaryngologist
    f. Oncologist
    g. Gynecologist
    h. Sports orthopedist
    i. Neurologist
    j. Urologist

The questions above underscore the importance of taking responsibility for your own health. How do you score? Here are the answers for questions 1 through 10:

    1. The Heimlich maneuver is performed when someone has swallowed something the wrong

way and is gasping for breath. The object can be liquid, solid food, or even a small solid. The person may be unable to breathe at all, and may start turning blue. Pull him or her to a standing position, with you behind the victim. Place your arms around him. Make one hand into a fist and place it on the other, just under the sternum. In one strong motion, press rapidly and VERY forcefully inward and upward, and the offending matter should come up and out. IMPORTANT: Do not be afraid to push with a force that could break a rib—it may be necessary. (Do not do the maneuver this way on babies or young children. Ask your pediatrician for special applications to children.)

My own daughter (where did I go wrong?) almost choked to death after swallowing a pill in her larynx, and neither she nor her husband had ever heard of the Heimlich. It's scary to start to choke to death, and after she recovered, she boned up on the maneuver.

The next time it happened, she swallowed a bolus of food the wrong way. Fortunately, a friend who was with her knew exactly what to do—and out popped the bolus!

2. Cardiopulmonary resuscitation (CPR). You're best off going to classes for this one. Contact your local Red Cross or hospital to find out about professional instruction. You may be able to save a life if you're trained.

3. If you haven't done so, ask your physician to do a complete cholesterol profile.

- Your total cholesterol should be under 200.
- Your HDL (the "good" cholesterol) should be between 40 and 60.
- Your LDL (the "bad" cholesterol) should be under 100.
- Your triglyceride should be less than 150.

If you're not within normal limits, do whatever your physician tells you to do to bring the numbers down. He or she may recommend a diet or possibly medicine, but it's important to follow the advice!

4. Don't panic if you have a dizzy spell ("vertigo" in the lingo). There are several factors that cause dizziness, but the first thing to do is to go to a neuro-otologist, who specializes in vestibular disorders (balance disorders). One is Menière's disease, which can also cause hearing loss in the ear affected. Symptoms include dizziness, ringing in the ear, and hearing loss. A neuro-otologist can control this with diet changes, medicine, or surgery.

Most common in older people is benign paroxysmal positional vertigo (BPPV). I have this, in spades. It started one morning when I got up from bed and immediately fell back, totally dizzy. After crawling to the bathroom, I called the doctor I know who is a vestibular expert, for an appointment. (**Note:** Know which doctor to call!) Friends took me to see her in a wheelchair because I was still unable to walk.

The doctor put me on the table, took my head, and maneuvered it for thirty seconds. And—mirabile dictu—I was cured and walked out of the office.

BPPV is caused by the little stones (calcium carbonate) in our ears that float in the jellylike space and allow us to balance ourselves. (Yes, we do have rocks in our heads!) When we get older, particularly if we have had any form of migraine, these stones cut loose and float into the wrong spaces, causing dizziness. The doctor's maneuvering of the head causes the rocks to float back where they belong, curing the dizziness. There are other causes of dizziness, which your physician can diagnose, but these two disorders are the most common.

5. The general symptoms of heart attack are:

- Uncomfortable chest pressure, fullness, squeezing, or pain that lasts longer than a few minutes
- Chest discomfort coupled with light-

headedness, fainting, sweating, nausea, or shortness of breath

- Pain radiating to shoulders, neck, and arms

Sometimes there are other signs, like stomach or abdominal pain, nausea or dizziness, trouble breathing, anxiety, weakness or fatigue, and palpitations, cold sweat, or paleness, and pain in the arm. Women, however, may have more subtle symptoms that indicate a heart attack. Fatigue and sleeplessness can be symptomatic of a heart attack's arrival. *Don't delay!* Call 911 immediately, and go to an emergency room for immediate hospitalization. Chew on an aspirin while waiting—it will help break up a blood clot. Time is of the essence!

6. Call 911 immediately if you have any of the following signs of a stroke:

- Sudden numbness or weakness in face, arm, or leg, especially on one side of the body

- Sudden confusion, trouble speaking, or understanding
- Sudden trouble seeing in one or both eyes
- Sudden trouble walking, dizziness, loss of balance or coordination, and sudden severe headache without known cause

There may be a difference in the way men and women perceive these symptoms: men may report changes in sensation and balance problems, while women often report headaches, disorientation, and pain in the face or limbs. Again, *don't delay!* The faster you get help, the less damage the stroke is likely to do. Call for emergency medical assistance if you have any of the warning signs or see them in another person. *You must be treated within three hours to assure the best recovery.* If you remember nothing else in this book, remember this!

7. Arthritis is just as sure to hit us as death and taxes. It is the most common of all diseases for older people (I am speaking of osteoarthritis, the age-related degenerative joint disease). It is absolutely essential that we deal with it, and then forget it, and get on with our lives. Every doctor seems to have a different arthritis cure. You simply have to find your own way through this problem.

One such problem was a tough one for me. As I've already said, I was as athletic as I could possibly be: exercising, playing tennis, skiing, swimming. Of course there would be flare-ups in my joints, especially my shoulder. My sports orthopod was willing to operate on the torn rotary cuff in my shoulder, but suggested I try therapy first. After four months of pulling those darn Therabands, the shoulder was usable. It still hurt, but if you want to live a full life, you have to get to a place where you can tolerate a certain degree of pain. I still do the Therabands, and it still hurts when I play tennis, but the rewards of being in the game are worth it.

Other crises would follow: first my thumbs gave me trouble, then a painful bursitis in my hips shut down any hopes of playing tennis. I tried acupuncture, cortisone injections, and pain drugs:

- Acupuncture seemed to help one side, but was unsuccessful on the other.
- Cortisone shots helped, of course, but one must limit this medication because cortisone stays in the body (it is not excreted) and that's evidently not good. No more than three shots!
- Pain drugs didn't really help.

Finally one doctor prescribed Vioxx, and *hallelujah*, it worked. I took Vioxx for four years until it was withdrawn because a study showed that it might cause heart attacks. After stopping taking it, I found that I was doing pretty well without it! My theory is that the Vioxx allowed me to exercise all my joints and subdued the arthritis.

So my advice for this kind of arthritis is: keep those joints moving, with all the exercises you can do. Exercise is the only long-term remedy for arthritis. To find the right doctor, go to a sports medicine orthopod—such doctors generally let you keep on doing what you want to do. As I have said, while I was getting my shoulder healed, my orthopod let me play tennis as long as I didn't raise my arm high while serving. I learned to do a low elbow twist serve: anything to keep going!

8. Alzheimer's disease is a tough one. As we grow older, we all become alarmed when we forget names, appointments, and things we have every intention of accomplishing. That does not mean that you are at risk for Alzheimer's. You may forget where you put your keys, but don't forget that when you were

much younger you had episodes exactly like that and thought nothing of it. Now that you're older, it becomes more significant, with the fear of Alzheimer's preoccupying you. If that is all that's bothering you, remember that we all get a condition called benign senescent forgetfulness. One thing we can do for it is to improve our attention (see Chapter 3).

Here's the $64,000 question: How can we tell if we or a loved one has Alzheimer's? It is said that it's all right to forget where you put your keys, but if you forget what your keys are for, that's Alzheimer's. There may be more subtle symptoms: forgetting how to do some simple arithmetic; becoming confused in driving around familiar streets; doing strange things like using a screwdriver to read the scales so they read what you expect them to. Or, as the nurses in my second husband's clinic found (he was an otolaryngologist by profession), he had forgotten what the drugs in the drug cabinet were for. He had to stop practicing after that, of course.

It's hard for me to talk about Alzheimer's. It tears you apart to see your spouse start on that long journey to oblivion. It's hard to know what will happen to you and your loved ones in life, so enjoy the time that you spend together.

9. Pulmonary (lung) problems are almost as common as arthritis. There are two fairly distinct conditions, with different causes:

Chronic obstructive pulmonary disease (COPD), otherwise known as smoker's lungs. I am seeing many of the senior population reap the "rewards" of having smoked when they were young. I'm one of them. It hit me when I was eighty, despite all the exercising I was doing. Yes, I began smoking when I was eighteen and quit when I was fifty-eight. I smoked two packs a day (with time off for three pregnancies and for breast-feeding). I think I'd be on oxygen if I hadn't exercised most of my life.

COPD is an umbrella term for conditions that obstruct air passages (bronchi) or damage the smaller air sacs (alveoli) in the lungs, resulting in progressively impaired breathing. Although irreversible, COPD is something one can live with if it is treated by a pulmonary specialist who may prescribe bronchodilators or oxygen. The doctor may also prescribe antibiotics to treat or to prevent bacterial lung infections.

Asthma. This is a condition caused by chronically hyperactive and inflamed airways, with occasional acute episodes of reversible narrowing of the airways. In other words, you can experience sudden difficulty breathing, a sense of suffocation, tightness in the chest, or coughing. There may be a hereditary predisposition to asthma.

Usually, asthma is caused by an allergy to some foreign substance, but may be precipitated by cold or dry air, smoke, bronchitis, vigorous exercise, emotional excitement, or stress. If you have asthma, you know that treatment includes a bronchodilator inhaler or bronchodilator drugs, corticosteroid pills, or desensitizing injections. In other words, asthma can be controlled with good treatment.

10. Typically, there are no symptoms of osteoporosis until there is gradual loss of height and stooping posture. There may also be lower back pain as a result of a vertebral fracture, or one may have a wrist or hip fracture. The disease is caused by an imbalance of bone formation and bone resorption, resulting in brittle bones that are susceptible to fracture. Most commonly it affects people over age seventy, and is four times more frequent in women than in men.

In addition to hereditary factors, other conditions place one at risk: being underweight, physical inactivity, excessive alcohol use, smoking, calcium deficiency, and reduced estrogen levels after menopause. Preventive measures include a diet rich in calcium (1,500 mg) and vitamin D (600 to 800 IU); regular weight-bearing exercise; and some form of estrogen replacement or compensation as advised by your doctor. Fortunately, treatment is effective, and your doctor may prescribe drug therapy that can slow bone resorption and even build bone. As ever, exercise is indicated to preserve function. Consider being screened for osteoporosis if you have a family history, are a woman over sixty-five, or have experienced a nontraumatic fracture.

I have had several bone density tests over the years to be sure that I can safely continue to ski, bicycle, play tennis—and skydive if I want! And the results have always been near the norms for a thirty-year-old, I'm embarrassed to say. I credit the fact that immediately after menopause I started hormone replacement, took calcium, and continued exercising religiously. So I have no fear as I land with a parachute!

FINDING THE RIGHT DOC

It started with just a little scruff of skin on the inside of my lower calf, then advanced very slowly into an open sore. Before long it became a white circle of rough skin, with a black center, and it kept growing until it was two inches in diameter. I went to see four separate doctors, and all of them said the same thing: "A spider bite." Indeed, it looked just like the picture of a spider bite I found on the Web, but it resisted any treatment that the doctors prescribed. Finally, in a long-distance call, my wonderful son-in-law suggested I try a wound clinic. There the doctors decided immediately to do something no one had thought of: a biopsy.

It turned out to be a squamous-cell carcinoma, which is one step this side of a melanoma, but still a malignant tumor that must be removed. Fortunately, the oncologist who removed it used a Mohs procedure; this meant that I was kept in the clinic until the doctors received the report that certified that they'd gotten all the cancer.

Q.E.D. Find the right doc!

At this time, it's hard for us oldies to get ANY medical attention at all, due to the vagaries of Medicare. If we're on Medicare, doctors lose money every time we step into their office. Have you noticed that they try to get rid of you as quickly as they can? Their care is not as thorough as it used to be, and we have suffered as a result. The hopeful sign is that there is a movement afoot to institute some sort of universal health care, which would cover us in the same way that the younger ones are covered. It would be a public system, paid for by taxes, which would amount to less than half of what we are paying for insurance now. *An end devoutly to be desired!*

One of the best ways to find the best doctor is to talk to paraprofessionals: the nurses, attendants, physical therapists, audiologists—anyone associated with medical doctors. *They know!* Your own doctor may not be a good source: my internist once referred me to an ear, nose, and throat doctor whom I, as an audiologist, knew to be one of the worst practitioners in the state. But evidently this man had referred patients to my doctor, and this was a quid pro quo situation: you rub my back, I'll rub yours. So before taking a referral, do your own checking. Ask the paraprofessionals. And if it's a surgeon who's being referred, find out how many operations of your kind he has performed in the last year.

Universal rule: *Ask, ask, ask!* Ask everybody you know. If you've had a diagnosis, don't be afraid to ask a doctor for a second opinion. In this case, choose your second doctor yourself. It's your prerogative as a patient: in fact, it's a legal right. Don't necessarily go to the man your doctor recommends; he may be a friend who will confirm the first diagnosis out of courtesy to his friend.

It is *very* important to find the right doc. There are horror stories about people whose doctors were not up to the latest medical knowledge of their problem. And there are also extraordinary stories about miraculous recoveries by people who found the right doctor.

There *are* primary doctors who are immensely knowledgeable about the appropriate state-of-the-art treatments for diseases, and will refer you to the appropriate specialists when indicated. I happen to know one very well, whom I would trust with my life because he is a brilliant diagnostician who also knows which specialists can do the job for you. He is the doctor who has engraved in his office the motto I've used to open Chapter 2: "Whatever the problem, exercise is always part of the solution." He cares avidly about prevention. As if you didn't know, an ounce of prevention . . . And, if you educate yourself about your particular disease or problem, you will be able to judge whether your doctor is up-to-date on all its aspects.

The Internet is a great source of credible information on health. For example, Harvard Medical School provides an editorial overview of the Aetna InteliHealth site at www.intelihealth.com. Another treasure trove is the website of the National Institutes of Health (nih.gov). And if you want the database of all the medical journals, the National Library of Medicine offers PubMed.

You can also become medically sophisticated by subscribing to one or more of the pamphlets that are put out monthly by a number of prominent medical institutions. Read, read, read about everything that is covered in these brochures. They represent the cutting edge of modern medicine. You'll be surprised at the extent of your ignorance about medicine, your attachment to old wives' tales, and your adherence to habits that can hurt you. Here are some sources that I've found useful:

The Johns Hopkins Medical Letter
Health After 50
P.O. Box 420179
Palm Coast FL 32141
www.hopkinsafter50.com

The Harvard Medical Letters
Harvard Health Publications
10 Shattuck Street, Suite 612
Boston MA 02115

Others: The University of California at Berkeley (Wellness), Mayo Clinic, and Cleveland Clinic newsletters.

Now that we've worried this topic to death, let me become the devil's advocate and say: the best thing is to let the body heal itself. All those billions of cells that inhabit your body want to be well just as ardently as you do. Always give them a chance.

Have you ever watched in awe as a wound slowly and stubbornly heals itself, until there are no signs left of the trauma that occurred? Have you imagined how those determined cells reach out to each other doggedly until at last they reach and unite as one? And while they're doing that, have you heard, as I have, the faint echo of Beethoven's Ninth Symphony in the background, with the chorale singing, *"Alle Menschen werden Brüdern"*—all men are brothers? All cells are brothers, too, and want to do their family duties.

A great doctor and researcher, Lewis Thomas, commented that doctors' families tend to complain that they receive less medical attention than their friends and neighbors yet they seem a normal, generally healthy lot, with a remarkably low incidence of iatrogenic (doctor-caused) illness. Lewis went on to say, "The great secret, known to internists and learned early in marriage by internists' wives but still hidden from the general public, is that most things get better by themselves. Most things, in fact, are better in the morning."

ON THE IMPORTANCE OF AN ADVOCATE

Hospitals are not hospitable places for the ol' bod'. Even the doctors know that. During my recent incarceration, one of the attending physicians told me: "I'd like to get you dismissed to go home just as soon as you can. All sorts of germs and viruses lurk around the corridors of hospitals, and the longer you are here, the better the chances are that one of them will get you."

So I made every effort to get well quickly, but it was slow going. While skiing I had cracked my sacrum (tailbone) in two places, and the pain was unbearable. The docs tried to ease my discomfort with medications of all sorts, most of which put me in a near-coma that precluded my eating anything, and I was allowed to drink only enough to keep me alive. I realized that, at ninety-three, I was actually very close to a premature (to me) death.

But I lucked out. All this time, I had two powerful advocates at my side: a daughter, and a friend who was a physician and a psychiatrist. They saw what was happening, and stopped the orders for what would have been an overdose of painkillers for an older person. They insisted that other medications be tried, and that I be moved to a rehab unit to try other means. Without the two of them, I don't think I would have made it.

In the rehab unit, the docs tried lesser medications until they found one that was a controlled substance, and could be kept under control. Soon I was able to exercise with a walker, and it was then that the good doc told me he wanted me out as soon as possible. At first my advocates resisted my going home, but after a long session with the doctor they agreed that it was time.

When I got home I had another advocate: my Marquis de Sade. He immediately made arrangements to take me every day to an indoor swimming pool, where I could use my legs to walk easily and get my muscles back in shape. Two weeks of that and I was water-logged, begging to get on with other exercises. The Marquis was merciless, of course, and he had me walking unassisted in a couple of weeks.

The moral of this story is simply that you must have an advocate if you find yourself hospital-bound. Choose someone who is medically sophisticated or who is willing to ask questions at every point. He or she would do well to go on the Web and find out all that is available about your particular problem, so the questions are relevant. The advocate also should be willing to stay at your side for the duration, even sleeping in your hospital room if possible.

Friends and/or family are the designated drivers here.

finding a good dentist

Let's sink our teeth into this problem: How do we look for a really good dentist? I wish I had thought of this fifty years ago, when my dentist decided he had to pull all four front teeth of mine, because I'd broken one off. Why all four, I don't know—all he had to do was cap them, or give me teeth implants if necessary. But I didn't know about those things then, so I let him yank out the perfectly good teeth and put in a bridge. The bridge led to decays of the adjacent teeth, and before I knew it, I had a full denture in my lower mouth.

The point is: First, I should have questioned the reason for such radical removal; and second, I should have asked for an outside consultation. At the time, the whole thing didn't feel good to me, but I never thought of fighting for myself. I do now, and you must engrave it in your mind: *If something doesn't feel right to you, don't allow it until and unless you have understood the reason for it, and have gotten another dentist's opinion.* The other dentist should be one you have chosen yourself, even if it's an expensive choice.

Trust your common sense: How do you feel about what is going on? Analyze whether the recommendation is a quick fix or a long-term solution. You're going to have to live with those teeth the rest of your life. Make sure they're good for the long haul. Though you may be tempted to choose temporary patches for dental problems, it might be better to invest in stronger materials that can last for decades. In dentistry, an ounce of prevention can be worth more than a pound of cure.

Choosing a dentist in the first place is another matter, and there are rules for that, too:

- Ask, ask, ask friends and family whom they would refer you to. Question their experiences with the dentists, and how they felt about his decisions.

- Never, never get a dentist from the yellow pages.
- Never, never get a dentist from ads on TV or in the paper without making inquiries. There's a lot of hype in those ads.
- Find out whether or when the prospective dentist has taken continuing education of some sort: fellowship, advanced training, or courses in dentistry. Dentists must keep up with their profession.

My favorite Internet search for finding a dentist is www.pankey.org. No hanky in that panky, just look for "Finding a Dentist."

And as if you didn't know, cut down on sugars, and brush regularly and correctly. There's a best way to brush; find out what it is.

death

I don't mind dying—I just don't want to be there
when it happens. —Woody Allen

No matter how good we are at surviving, there's
always death. People have been afraid of death
since primitive times; that's why religions have stayed
with us so long—it's the only way we can "live forever."
But you still can't avoid death. We envision our dying
as an agonizing, wrenching time; "Don't let me die—
please let me live longer—I'm afraid of that last
breath." Rather than think that, wouldn't this be a
better approach: "As long as I can think, I'm still

alive, and I will be alive until that last moment. After that, who cares?"

Nature has provided in minute detail how we are to be born, how we develop into mature organisms, how we move and sustain our bodies. Isn't it logical that nature will have provided for the way we die? From accounts of people who've had a go-round with death and a near-dying experience, and survived it, the experience was quite peaceful and tranquil.

Lewis Thomas, the former Harvard researcher, believes that there is a mechanism that eliminates pain when death is imminent. He cites the case of a mouse that is caught by a cat and mangled, and while still alive is carried around in the cat's mouth. At first the mouse squeals, but when death is imminent, there seems to be no pain, and the mouse seems resigned and happy to die. It's a rather morbid tale, but if Thomas thinks there is an analogy to humans, I'm for it.

My granddaughter Emily suffered a life-threatening brain tumor, and several years later, I also had a brain tumor. Her poem "Turquoise Bloom," which she wrote to commemorate the fact that neither of us had been apprehensive about having surgery, ended like this:

The fear of death is not worth
The cost of a frightened life.

Fear is the enemy. A friend of mine was afraid to die. He had an inordinate fear of wild animals; he was obsessive about locking doors; he accumulated an arsenal of guns to protect himself against imagined attacks; he spent his whole life bypassing dangerous situations. The fear finally drove him to invest in expensive channelers (those who produced "Seth" gave him assurance of future life) and mind sciences that elevate the mind above the body. His life was wasted in large part because of his fear of death. Unfortunately, he was not a devout Christian, and didn't have the comfort of a belief in life after death. That might have helped him.

Death is a consequence of life. More than 50 million of us humans die each year. Most of those deaths are viewed as catastrophes; they are mourned and cried over, ceremonialized and flower-showered, without being recognized as part of the other 49,999,999 who are accompanying them to wherever their families think they are going.

Lewis Thomas tells a story about squirrels that illustrates this point:

> I have lived all my life with an embarrassment of squirrels in my backyard. They are all over the place, all year long, and I have never seen, anywhere, a dead squirrel. . . . If all the dying were done in the open, with the dead lying everywhere to be looked at, we would never have it out of our minds.

The fact that death—of squirrels and of humans—happens in relative secrecy makes the process of dying appear to be more exceptional than it really is, and harder to engage in at the times when we must ourselves engage. It's time we stopped aggrandizing death and accepted it for what it is—a natural part of the life cycle of all of us! We should take comfort in the fact that somewhere a replacement for us is being born—we may even get twofers!

For some of us, it doesn't matter whether there is life after death—this wonderful life is quite sufficient. We are a part of the evolution of the earth, and we are one with all living creatures. We accept death as a part of that evolution, and we are content. While we're here, we should live it up!

Addendum: Some of you may have drawn up a living will, which is a limited directive for end-of-life wishes. However, if you desire more stringent instructions, you may elect to write out further, more specific directions for your physician and your family. You may like to follow the kind of directions I have proposed, as follows:

TO THE PHYSICIAN IN CHARGE OF MY CASE

In addition to the stipulations in the legal living will that I have executed, I would like to request further actions on the part of those responsible for my welfare. I know that many of my requests are not tolerated in the courts today, but I am hoping that by the time I die the courts will have become more merciful, allowing physicians also to be more merciful.

I request that, in addition to the passive withdrawal of life supports in the event of my being in the states described in the living will, you, or any or all of my children in concert, administer in any feasible way a medicine or procedure that will terminate my life. I also request that termination be accomplished not only when the conditions described in the living will prevail, but also under the following conditions:

When, following a stroke or onset of dementia of any type, or any other illness, I am unable, after a reasonable allowance for recovery (no more than six months):

to initiate propositional speech meaningfully, not only for concrete ideas but also for high abstractions, or to read a professional article and discuss it with clear understanding,

or to take care of my personal needs, including dressing, toilet, cooking, cleaning, etc.,

or to think cogently, because of mind-dulling drugs that have been administered for severe and unabating pain,

at the very least, I instruct that under the above conditions, no resuscitation be performed, all life support be stopped, no intravenous feeding or corporal or rectal clysis be performed, no gastric or nasal-gastric feeding be given, and that the only medication administered be morphine sulphate by injection, at 15 mg every two to three hours.

If at any time during the course of such disease I ask to be kept alive it will be because, as a result of the debilitating illness, I will no longer be the same person I have been for all the preceding years of my life. That changed person is not one I choose to perpetuate. I am a very proud woman, and also a very determined one. I have enjoyed my life as few people have, I believe, and the thought that the quality of my life would be so poor as to be a burden to myself and to my children is simply anathema to me.

I am writing this because, in court cases that have bordered on the kind of actions I am specifying here, it has seemed important what the individual's prior wishes were, and what kind of a person he/she was.

My three children are in complete agreement with my requests, and have promised to comply with my wishes if it is at all possible to do so. They also know that I would not want to put them in a position where court action might be taken against them, nor would I expect you to be put in such a position. I am involving my children because I am absolutely certain of their love for me and their wishes to abide by my requests. I also know that they are certain of my love for them, and that I would not want them to come to any harm because of me.

I hope this doesn't place too much of a burden on you. I have full faith and confidence in you to do the very best in my interest. I have merely tried to let you know what that interest is.

Sincerely,

Marion P. Downs, M.A., DHS, Hon. D.Sc., Professor Emerita, UCHSC

We, the following friends or relatives of Marion Downs, testify that the above requests have been discussed with her for years, and we verify that these are the true tenets of her life.

[signed]

CHAPTER 8

marion's
medical miscellany

- Sleep every night with a hard pillow between your knees. It prevents back trouble. It has kept my hip bursitis from coming back.
- If you have reflux (the surging up of stomach acid, or heartburn), lie on your left side. No doctor will tell you this, but everyone I know knows that lying on your left side will help prevent reflux. It's something about your stomach's position in your body.

I never knew that reflux could cause a chronic cough, even when one is not aware of having reflux. When I developed a nagging chronic cough, I attributed it to my COPD, and wondered why the doctors always asked if I had reflux. Their questions finally got through to me, and I tried a common over-the-counter stomach pill. The next day I had no cough, nor in successive days, as long as I took the pill. So, I'm cured of that problem, but I have been advised to see a gastroenterologist to be sure there has been no damage to my esophagus from the silent reflux. I will do so, as I know that one of the nastiest things to die from is cancer of the esophagus, and it turns out that half of chronic coughs are from silent reflux.

Moral: Listen carefully to what your doctor says.

- Incontinence creeps up on you when you get older, more often for women than for men, I believe. In my seventies, I had my bladder tied up, which also required a hysterectomy—and was pretty well relieved. More recently, I have difficulty, especially at those last moments when I'm on my way to the john. This is called—appropriately—"urgency." So, because of those moments, I resort to a pad. Well, we did it once, didn't we, girls?

· One of my medical descendants (an in-law) suggests a regimen of training the bladder: for four days, urinate every hour; next four days, every two hours; the next four days, three hours, and so on until you've trained the blad-der to last as long as you want it to. I haven't tried it, but it's worth giving it a try.

There are exercises (called Kegel) that are sup-posed to do the trick, too, but only if you do them every day. I've tried, but somehow my mind blocks and I forget to do them. Tomorrow I'll try to do them again.

· Women shouldn't take the daily minimum amount of aspirin that's recommended for men until they've consulted their doctors.

The definitive research has been completed at the Harvard School of Public Health. They studied **40,000** healthy women to determine the effects of aspirin, and have found that aspirin does help prevent strokes and heart attacks in women, but only for those whose doctors recommend the regimen for them. There are caveats for some women.

- And a word about my specialty: hearing! I would urge all people to consider using hearing aids at the first sign that they're not hearing as well as they used to. These signs include:

  - turning on the TV louder than other people want to have it
  - saying "What?" more than twice a day to your spouse or live-in
  - asking people to speak more slowly, or more distinctly, or louder

- finding that your spouse is speaking louder to you, which makes him or her sound angry

That last sign is important, as it can ruin a marriage. Raising one's voice makes one sound angry, and when anger comes into a marriage, it's hard to handle. I suddenly found in my marriage that my husband and I were shouting at each other, resulting in bad feelings on both sides. We each got a hearing aid, and life became pleasant again.

Statistically, men resist wearing hearing aids more than women do. Their macho vanity makes them feel that if they don't wear hearing aids, they will seem younger. What they don't realize is that nothing makes them seem older than constantly saying "What?" or losing the trend of the conversation.

Just be sure to go to a certified audiologist to get hearing aids. University centers are good places to find competitive prices for aids, and many audiologists now have Au.D. degrees, which are clinical doctorate degrees. Just remember to try out the aids for a month before you buy them, and if they're not right for you, try another brand. *It's required legally* that you can try them.

Also get aids for both ears—the binaural advantage in hearing is significant. You can demonstrate that fact by occluding one ear with your finger, pressing tightly against the ear flap (tragus), then listening to TV, or to someone talking, and find the difference between one and two ears!

Remember: If you lose your hearing, you lose your connection to other people, which is guaranteed to make you seem and feel . . . old.

I have been privileged to live in what is, up to now, the greatest era of discovery of all time. We have finally begun to understand such things as the structure of the cosmos, the nature of intelligence, myth and legend, birth and death, life beyond the earth, robots, climates, the makeup of the body, and the cells' most minute organization. As Lewis Thomas has said, "Most fortunate has been medicine's understanding of how to prevent diseases, and its great strides in curing them."

I have witnessed the great compassion that mankind

is capable of: tender caring for children who are ill, starving, or mistreated; striving to eliminate poverty and crime; love for family and friends. And yet, I grieve to see that man continues to kill man during all this time of enlightenment in science and life. I have lived through some six wars, minor and major, and I still view them as senseless in a world where we know better. Whether through religion or common sense, we know that it is not acceptable to hurt or kill others, because we do not want to be hurt or killed ourselves.

Religions have failed to prevent these man-made catastrophes. Can science accomplish it? Can scientific education become so pervasive that we will all become of one mind and forswear our own destruction?

I have no answers. Only questions.

Marion Downs worked for forty years to convince professionals to adopt newborn hearing screening in delivery hospitals. She says, "First they ignored me, then they laughed at me, then they ridiculed me, THEN I WON!" As a result of her work, ninety percent of all newborns in America are screened for hearing loss. She is Distinguished Professor Emerita in the Department of Otolaryngology, Division of Audiology, at the University of Colorado Health Sciences Center. She has written numerous professional books, articles, and chapters.

The Marion Downs Hearing Center (MDHC) at the University of Colorado Hospital and Health Sciences Center in Aurora, Colorado, was created to honor the legacy of Marion Downs. The center provides resources, education, and research to support the needs of individuals who are deaf and hard of hearing, their families, the community, and hearing health professionals. It values individual and family rights in communication and technology choices, and strives to optimize the quality of life for all it serves. The Marion Downs Hearing Center is recognized worldwide for its unique leadership and progressive innovations in the realm of hearing and deafness.

The Marion Downs Hearing Center Foundation supports the activities of the center and is currently in a capital campaign to raise necessary funding to build a new, state-of-the-art facility for its unique programs. For more information or to find out how you can be a part of this exciting venture, e-mail us at mdhc@uch.edu or access our website at www.mdhcfoundation.org.